This planner belongs to:

**NAME**

______________________________

**CONTACT INFORMATION**

______________________________

______________________________

______________________________

# 2021

**January 2021**

| S | M | T | W | T | F | S |
|---|---|---|---|---|---|---|
| | | | | | 1 | 2 |
| 3 | 4 | 5 | 6 | 7 | 8 | 9 |
| 10 | 11 | 12 | 13 | 14 | 15 | 16 |
| 17 | 18 | 19 | 20 | 21 | 22 | 23 |
| 24/31 | 25 | 26 | 27 | 28 | 29 | 30 |

**February 2021**

| S | M | T | W | T | F | S |
|---|---|---|---|---|---|---|
| | 1 | 2 | 3 | 4 | 5 | 6 |
| 7 | 8 | 9 | 10 | 11 | 12 | 13 |
| 14 | 15 | 16 | 17 | 18 | 19 | 20 |
| 21 | 22 | 23 | 24 | 25 | 26 | 27 |
| 28 | | | | | | |

**March 2021**

| S | M | T | W | T | F | S |
|---|---|---|---|---|---|---|
| | 1 | 2 | 3 | 4 | 5 | 6 |
| 7 | 8 | 9 | 10 | 11 | 12 | 13 |
| 14 | 15 | 16 | 17 | 18 | 19 | 20 |
| 21 | 22 | 23 | 24 | 25 | 26 | 27 |
| 28 | 29 | 30 | 31 | | | |

**April 2021**

| S | M | T | W | T | F | S |
|---|---|---|---|---|---|---|
| | | | | 1 | 2 | 3 |
| 4 | 5 | 6 | 7 | 8 | 9 | 10 |
| 11 | 12 | 13 | 14 | 15 | 16 | 17 |
| 18 | 19 | 20 | 21 | 22 | 23 | 24 |
| 25 | 26 | 27 | 28 | 29 | 30 | |

**May 2021**

| S | M | T | W | T | F | S |
|---|---|---|---|---|---|---|
| | | | | | | 1 |
| 2 | 3 | 4 | 5 | 6 | 7 | 8 |
| 9 | 10 | 11 | 12 | 13 | 14 | 15 |
| 16 | 17 | 18 | 19 | 20 | 21 | 22 |
| 23/30 | 24/31 | 25 | 26 | 27 | 28 | 29 |

**June 2021**

| S | M | T | W | T | F | S |
|---|---|---|---|---|---|---|
| | | 1 | 2 | 3 | 4 | 5 |
| 6 | 7 | 8 | 9 | 10 | 11 | 12 |
| 13 | 14 | 15 | 16 | 17 | 18 | 19 |
| 20 | 21 | 22 | 23 | 24 | 25 | 26 |
| 27 | 28 | 29 | 30 | | | |

**July 2021**

| S | M | T | W | T | F | S |
|---|---|---|---|---|---|---|
| | | | | 1 | 2 | 3 |
| 4 | 5 | 6 | 7 | 8 | 9 | 10 |
| 11 | 12 | 13 | 14 | 15 | 16 | 17 |
| 18 | 19 | 20 | 21 | 22 | 23 | 24 |
| 25 | 26 | 27 | 28 | 29 | 30 | 31 |

**August 2021**

| S | M | T | W | T | F | S |
|---|---|---|---|---|---|---|
| 1 | 2 | 3 | 4 | 5 | 6 | 7 |
| 8 | 9 | 10 | 11 | 12 | 13 | 14 |
| 15 | 16 | 17 | 18 | 19 | 20 | 21 |
| 22 | 23 | 24 | 25 | 26 | 27 | 28 |
| 29 | 30 | 31 | | | | |

**September 2021**

| S | M | T | W | T | F | S |
|---|---|---|---|---|---|---|
| | | | 1 | 2 | 3 | 4 |
| 5 | 6 | 7 | 8 | 9 | 10 | 11 |
| 12 | 13 | 14 | 15 | 16 | 17 | 18 |
| 19 | 20 | 21 | 22 | 23 | 24 | 25 |
| 26 | 27 | 28 | 29 | 30 | | |

**October 2021**

| S | M | T | W | T | F | S |
|---|---|---|---|---|---|---|
| | | | | | 1 | 2 |
| 3 | 4 | 5 | 6 | 7 | 8 | 9 |
| 10 | 11 | 12 | 13 | 14 | 15 | 16 |
| 17 | 18 | 19 | 20 | 21 | 22 | 23 |
| 24/31 | 25 | 26 | 27 | 28 | 29 | 30 |

**November 2021**

| S | M | T | W | T | F | S |
|---|---|---|---|---|---|---|
| | 1 | 2 | 3 | 4 | 5 | 6 |
| 7 | 8 | 9 | 10 | 11 | 12 | 13 |
| 14 | 15 | 16 | 17 | 18 | 19 | 20 |
| 21 | 22 | 23 | 24 | 25 | 26 | 27 |
| 28 | 29 | 30 | | | | |

**December 2021**

| S | M | T | W | T | F | S |
|---|---|---|---|---|---|---|
| | | | 1 | 2 | 3 | 4 |
| 5 | 6 | 7 | 8 | 9 | 10 | 11 |
| 12 | 13 | 14 | 15 | 16 | 17 | 18 |
| 19 | 20 | 21 | 22 | 23 | 24 | 25 |
| 26 | 27 | 28 | 29 | 30 | 31 | |

**January 2022**

| S | M | T | W | T | F | S |
|---|---|---|---|---|---|---|
| | | | | | | 1 |
| 2 | 3 | 4 | 5 | 6 | 7 | 8 |
| 9 | 10 | 11 | 12 | 13 | 14 | 15 |
| 16 | 17 | 18 | 19 | 20 | 21 | 22 |
| 23/30 | 24/31 | 25 | 26 | 27 | 28 | 29 |

**February 2022**

| S | M | T | W | T | F | S |
|---|---|---|---|---|---|---|
| | | 1 | 2 | 3 | 4 | 5 |
| 6 | 7 | 8 | 9 | 10 | 11 | 12 |
| 13 | 14 | 15 | 16 | 17 | 18 | 19 |
| 20 | 21 | 22 | 23 | 24 | 25 | 26 |
| 27 | 28 | | | | | |

**March 2022**

| S | M | T | W | T | F | S |
|---|---|---|---|---|---|---|
| | | 1 | 2 | 3 | 4 | 5 |
| 6 | 7 | 8 | 9 | 10 | 11 | 12 |
| 13 | 14 | 15 | 16 | 17 | 18 | 19 |
| 20 | 21 | 22 | 23 | 24 | 25 | 26 |
| 27 | 28 | 29 | 30 | 31 | | |

**April 2022**

| S | M | T | W | T | F | S |
|---|---|---|---|---|---|---|
| | | | | | 1 | 2 |
| 3 | 4 | 5 | 6 | 7 | 8 | 9 |
| 10 | 11 | 12 | 13 | 14 | 15 | 16 |
| 17 | 18 | 19 | 20 | 21 | 22 | 23 |
| 24 | 25 | 26 | 27 | 28 | 29 | 30 |

**May 2022**

| S | M | T | W | T | F | S |
|---|---|---|---|---|---|---|
| 1 | 2 | 3 | 4 | 5 | 6 | 7 |
| 8 | 9 | 10 | 11 | 12 | 13 | 14 |
| 15 | 16 | 17 | 18 | 19 | 20 | 21 |
| 22 | 23 | 24 | 25 | 26 | 27 | 28 |
| 29 | 30 | 31 | | | | |

**June 2022**

| S | M | T | W | T | F | S |
|---|---|---|---|---|---|---|
| | | | 1 | 2 | 3 | 4 |
| 5 | 6 | 7 | 8 | 9 | 10 | 11 |
| 12 | 13 | 14 | 15 | 16 | 17 | 18 |
| 19 | 20 | 21 | 22 | 23 | 24 | 25 |
| 26 | 27 | 28 | 29 | 30 | | |

**July 2022**

| S | M | T | W | T | F | S |
|---|---|---|---|---|---|---|
| | | | | | 1 | 2 |
| 3 | 4 | 5 | 6 | 7 | 8 | 9 |
| 10 | 11 | 12 | 13 | 14 | 15 | 16 |
| 17 | 18 | 19 | 20 | 21 | 22 | 23 |
| 24/31 | 25 | 26 | 27 | 28 | 29 | 30 |

**August 2022**

| S | M | T | W | T | F | S |
|---|---|---|---|---|---|---|
| | 1 | 2 | 3 | 4 | 5 | 6 |
| 7 | 8 | 9 | 10 | 11 | 12 | 13 |
| 14 | 15 | 16 | 17 | 18 | 19 | 20 |
| 21 | 22 | 23 | 24 | 25 | 26 | 27 |
| 28 | 29 | 30 | 31 | | | |

**September 2022**

| S | M | T | W | T | F | S |
|---|---|---|---|---|---|---|
| | | | | 1 | 2 | 3 |
| 4 | 5 | 6 | 7 | 8 | 9 | 10 |
| 11 | 12 | 13 | 14 | 15 | 16 | 17 |
| 18 | 19 | 20 | 21 | 22 | 23 | 24 |
| 25 | 26 | 27 | 28 | 29 | 30 | |

**October 2022**

| S | M | T | W | T | F | S |
|---|---|---|---|---|---|---|
| | | | | | | 1 |
| 2 | 3 | 4 | 5 | 6 | 7 | 8 |
| 9 | 10 | 11 | 12 | 13 | 14 | 15 |
| 16 | 17 | 18 | 19 | 20 | 21 | 22 |
| 23/30 | 24/31 | 25 | 26 | 27 | 28 | 29 |

**November 2022**

| S | M | T | W | T | F | S |
|---|---|---|---|---|---|---|
| | | 1 | 2 | 3 | 4 | 5 |
| 6 | 7 | 8 | 9 | 10 | 11 | 12 |
| 13 | 14 | 15 | 16 | 17 | 18 | 19 |
| 20 | 21 | 22 | 23 | 24 | 25 | 26 |
| 27 | 28 | 29 | 30 | | | |

**December 2022**

| S | M | T | W | T | F | S |
|---|---|---|---|---|---|---|
| | | | | 1 | 2 | 3 |
| 4 | 5 | 6 | 7 | 8 | 9 | 10 |
| 11 | 12 | 13 | 14 | 15 | 16 | 17 |
| 18 | 19 | 20 | 21 | 22 | 23 | 24 |
| 25 | 26 | 27 | 28 | 29 | 30 | 31 |

# HOLIDAYS

| | 2021 | 2022 |
|---|---|---|
| New Year's Day | Jan. 1 | Jan. 1 |
| Holiday (Scot., N.Z.) | Jan. 4 | Jan. 4 |
| Epiphany | Jan. 6 | Jan. 6 |
| Orthodox Christmas Day | Jan. 7 | Jan. 7 |
| Orthodox New Year | Jan. 14 | Jan. 14 |
| Martin Luther King, Jr. Day (U.S.) | Jan. 18 | Jan. 17 |
| Australia Day | Jan. 26 | Jan. 26 |
| Groundhog Day (U.S., CA) | Feb. 2 | Feb. 2 |
| Constitution Day (MX) | Feb. 5 | Feb. 5 |
| Waitangi Day (N.Z.) | Feb. 6 | Feb. 6 |
| Chinese New Year begins | Feb. 12 | Feb. 1 |
| Lincoln's Birthday (U.S.) | Feb. 12 | Feb. 12 |
| Valentine's Day | Feb. 14 | Feb. 14 |
| Presidents' Day/Washington's Birthday (U.S.) | Feb. 15 | Feb. 21 |
| Shrove Tuesday/Mardi Gras | Feb. 16 | Mar. 1 |
| Ash Wednesday | Feb. 17 | Mar. 2 |
| Purim (begins at sundown) | Feb. 25 | Mar. 17 |
| International Women's Day | Mar. 8 | Mar. 8 |
| Daylight Saving Time begins (U.S., CA) | Mar. 14 | Mar. 13 |
| St. Patrick's Day | Mar. 17 | Mar. 17 |
| March Equinox | Mar. 20 | Mar. 20 |
| Mother's Day (U.K., Rep. of Ire.) | Mar. 14 | Mar. 27 |
| Passover (begins at sundown) | Mar. 27 | Apr. 15 |
| Palm Sunday | Mar. 28 | Apr. 10 |
| British/European Summer Time begins | Mar. 28 | Mar. 27 |
| April Fools' Day | Apr. 1 | Apr. 1 |
| Good Friday | Apr. 2 | Apr. 15 |
| Daylight Saving Time ends (AU) | Apr. 4 | Apr. 3 |
| Easter Sunday | Apr. 4 | Apr. 17 |
| Easter Monday | Apr. 5 | Apr. 18 |
| Holocaust Remembrance Day (begins at sundown) | Apr. 7 | Apr. 27 |
| Ramadan (begins at sundown) | Apr. 12 | Apr. 2 |
| Income Tax Due (U.S.) | Apr. 15 | Apr. 18 |
| Earth Day | Apr. 22 | Apr. 22 |
| ANZAC Day (AU, N.Z.) | Apr. 25 | Apr. 25 |
| King's Birthday (NL) | Apr. 27 | Apr. 27 |
| May Day | May 1 | May 1 |
| Constitution Day (PL) | May 3 | May 3 |
| Holiday (U.K., Rep. of Ire.) | May 3 | May 2 |
| Cinco de Mayo (U.S., MX) | May 5 | May 5 |
| Liberation Day (NL) | May 5 | May 5 |
| Laylat al-Qadr (begins at sundown) | May 8 | Apr. 27 |
| Mother's Day (U.S., CA, AU) | May 9 | May 8 |
| Eid al-Fitr (begins at sundown) | May 12 | May 2 |
| Victoria Day (CA) | May 24 | May 23 |
| Memorial Day (U.S.) | May 31 | May 30 |
| Holiday (U.K.) | May 31 | May 30 |
| Holiday (Rep. of Ire.) | June 7 | June 6 |
| Queen's Birthday (N.Z.) | June 7 | June 6 |
| Queen's Birthday (AU) | June 14 | June 13 |
| Flag Day (U.S.) | June 14 | June 14 |

| | | |
|---|---|---|
| Father's Day (U.S., CA, U.K.) | June 20 | June 19 |
| June Solstice | June 21 | June 21 |
| Canada Day | July 1 | July 1 |
| Independence Day (U.S.) | July 4 | July 4 |
| Holiday (N. Ire.) | July 12 | July 12 |
| Bastille Day (FR) | July 14 | July 14 |
| Eid al-Adha (begins at sundown) | July 19 | July 9 |
| Holiday (CA, Scot., Rep. of Ire.) | Aug. 2 | Aug. 1 |
| Al-Hijra (begins at sundown) | Aug. 9 | July 29 |
| Holiday (Eng., N. Ire., Wales) | Aug. 30 | Aug. 29 |
| Labor Day (U.S., CA) | Sept. 6 | Sept. 5 |
| Rosh Hashanah (begins at sundown) | Sept. 6 | Sept. 25 |
| Patriot Day (U.S.) | Sept. 11 | Sept. 11 |
| Grandparents Day (U.S.) | Sept. 12 | Sept. 11 |
| Yom Kippur (begins at sundown) | Sept. 15 | Oct. 4 |
| Independence Day (MX) | Sept. 16 | Sept. 16 |
| Constitution Day/Citizenship Day (U.S.) | Sept. 17 | Sept. 17 |
| International Day of Peace | Sept. 21 | Sept. 21 |
| September Equinox | Sept. 22 | Sept. 22 |
| Daylight Saving Time begins (AU) | Oct. 3 | Oct. 2 |
| Labour Day (AU) | Oct. 4 | Oct. 3 |
| Columbus Day (U.S.) | Oct. 11 | Oct. 10 |
| Thanksgiving Day (CA) | Oct. 11 | Oct. 10 |
| Holiday (Rep. of Ire.) | Oct. 25 | Oct. 31 |
| Labour Day (N.Z.) | Oct. 25 | Oct. 24 |
| Halloween | Oct. 31 | Oct. 31 |
| British/European Summer Time ends | Oct. 31 | Oct. 30 |
| All Saints' Day | Nov. 1 | Nov. 1 |
| All Souls' Day | Nov. 2 | Nov. 2 |
| Election Day (U.S.) | Nov. 2 | Nov. 8 |
| Guy Fawkes Night (U.K.) | Nov. 5 | Nov. 5 |
| Daylight Saving Time ends (U.S., CA) | Nov. 7 | Nov. 6 |
| Veterans/Remembrance/ArmisticeDay | Nov. 11 | Nov. 11 |
| Independence Day (PL) | Nov. 11 | Nov. 11 |
| Remembrance Sunday (U.K.) | Nov. 14 | Nov. 13 |
| Revolution Day (MX) | Nov. 20 | Nov. 20 |
| Thanksgiving Day (U.S.) | Nov. 25 | Nov. 24 |
| Hanukkah (begins at sundown) | Nov. 28 | Dec. 18 |
| Advent begins | Nov. 28 | Nov. 27 |
| St. Andrew's Day (Scot.) | Nov. 30 | Nov. 30 |
| World AIDS Day | Dec. 1 | Dec. 1 |
| Pearl Harbor Remembrance Day (U.S.) | Dec. 7 | Dec. 7 |
| December Solstice | Dec. 21 | Dec. 21 |
| Christmas Eve | Dec. 24 | Dec. 24 |
| Christmas Day | Dec. 25 | Dec. 25 |
| First Day of Kwanzaa | Dec. 26 | Dec. 26 |
| Boxing Day | Dec. 26 | Dec. 26 |
| New Year's Eve | Dec. 31 | Dec. 31 |

| NOTES | SUNDAY | MONDAY | TUESDAY |
|---|---|---|---|
| | 27 | 28 | 29 |
| | 3 | 4<br>Holiday (Scot., N.Z.) | 5 |
| | 10 | 11 | 12 |
| | 17 | 18<br>Martin Luther King, Jr. Day (U.S.) | 19 |
| | 24 | 25<br>Burns' Night (Scot.) | 26<br>Australia Day |
| | 31 | 1 | 2 |

DECEMBER 2020

| S | M | T | W | T | F | S |
|---|---|---|---|---|---|---|
| | | 1 | 2 | 3 | 4 | 5 |
| 6 | 7 | 8 | 9 | 10 | 11 | 12 |
| 13 | 14 | 15 | 16 | 17 | 18 | 19 |
| 20 | 21 | 22 | 23 | 24 | 25 | 26 |
| 27 | 28 | 29 | 30 | 31 | | |

FEBRUARY

| S | M | T | W | T | F | S |
|---|---|---|---|---|---|---|
| | 1 | 2 | 3 | 4 | 5 | 6 |
| 7 | 8 | 9 | 10 | 11 | 12 | 13 |
| 14 | 15 | 16 | 17 | 18 | 19 | 20 |
| 21 | 22 | 23 | 24 | 25 | 26 | 27 |
| 28 | | | | | | |

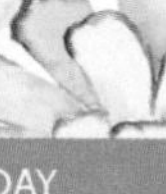

# January 2021

| WEDNESDAY | THURSDAY | FRIDAY | SATURDAY |
| --- | --- | --- | --- |
| 0 | 31 | 1<br>New Year's Day | 2 |
| Epiphany<br>Last Quarter ◑ | 7<br>Orthodox Christmas Day | 8 | 9 |
| 3<br>New Moon ● | 14<br>Orthodox New Year | 15 | 16 |
| 0<br>First Quarter ◐ | 21 | 22 | 23 |
| 7 | 28<br>Full Moon ○ | 29 | 30 |
| | 4 | 5 | 6 |

| NOTES | SUNDAY | MONDAY | TUESDAY |
|---|---|---|---|
| | 31 | 1<br>Start of Black History Month (U.S., CA)<br>National Freedom Day (U.S.) | 2<br>Groundhog Day (U.S., CA) |
| | 7<br>Super Bowl Sunday (U.S.) | 8<br>Waitangi Day observed (N.Z.) | 9 |
| | 14<br>Valentine's Day | 15<br>Presidents' Day/ Washington's Birthday (U.S.) | 16<br>Shrove Tuesday/ Mardi Gras |
| | 21 | 22 | 23 |
| | 28 | 1 | 2 |
| | 7 | 8 | 9 |

JANUARY

| S | M | T | W | T | F | S |
|---|---|---|---|---|---|---|
| | | | | | 1 | 2 |
| 3 | 4 | 5 | 6 | 7 | 8 | 9 |
| 10 | 11 | 12 | 13 | 14 | 15 | 16 |
| 17 | 18 | 19 | 20 | 21 | 22 | 23 |
| 24 | 25 | 26 | 27 | 28 | 29 | 30 |
| 31 | | | | | | |

MARCH

| S | M | T | W | T | F | S |
|---|---|---|---|---|---|---|
| | 1 | 2 | 3 | 4 | 5 | 6 |
| 7 | 8 | 9 | 10 | 11 | 12 | 13 |
| 14 | 15 | 16 | 17 | 18 | 19 | 20 |
| 21 | 22 | 23 | 24 | 25 | 26 | 27 |
| 28 | 29 | 30 | 31 | | | |

# February 2021

| WEDNESDAY | THURSDAY | FRIDAY | SATURDAY |
|---|---|---|---|
| | 4<br>Last Quarter ◑ | 5<br>Constitution Day (MX) | 6<br>Waitangi Day (N.Z.) |
| | 11<br>New Moon ● | 12<br>Chinese New Year begins (Year of the Ox)<br>Lincoln's Birthday (U.S.) | 13 |
| Ash Wednesday | 18 | 19<br>First Quarter ◐ | 20 |
| | 25<br>Purim (begins at sundown) | 26 | 27<br>Full Moon ○ |
| | 4 | 5 | 6 |
| | 11 | 12 | 13 |

| NOTES | SUNDAY | MONDAY | TUESDAY |
|---|---|---|---|
| | 28 | 1<br>Start of Women's History Month (U.S., U.K., AU)<br>St. David's Day | 2 |
| | 7 | 8<br>International Women's Day<br>Commonwealth Day (CA, U.K., AU) | 9 |
| | 14<br>Daylight Saving Time begins (U.S., CA)<br>Mother's Day (U.K., Rep. of Ire.) | 15 | 16 |
| | 21<br>First Quarter ◐ | 22 | 23 |
| | 28<br>Palm Sunday<br>British/European Summer Time begins<br>Full Moon ○ | 29 | 30 |
| | 4 | 5 | 6 |

FEBRUARY

| S | M | T | W | T | F | S |
|---|---|---|---|---|---|---|
| | 1 | 2 | 3 | 4 | 5 | 6 |
| 7 | 8 | 9 | 10 | 11 | 12 | 13 |
| 14 | 15 | 16 | 17 | 18 | 19 | 20 |
| 21 | 22 | 23 | 24 | 25 | 26 | 27 |
| 28 | | | | | | |

APRIL

| S | M | T | W | T | F | S |
|---|---|---|---|---|---|---|
| | | | | 1 | 2 | 3 |
| 4 | 5 | 6 | 7 | 8 | 9 | 10 |
| 11 | 12 | 13 | 14 | 15 | 16 | 17 |
| 18 | 19 | 20 | 21 | 22 | 23 | 24 |
| 25 | 26 | 27 | 28 | 29 | 30 | |

# March 2021

| VEDNESDAY | THURSDAY | FRIDAY | SATURDAY |
|---|---|---|---|
| | 4 | 5 | 6<br>Last Quarter ◑ |
| o | 11 | 12 | 13<br>New Moon ● |
| 7<br>St. Patrick's Day | 18 | 19 | 20<br>March Equinox |
| 4 | 25 | 26 | 27<br>Passover<br>(begins at sundown) |
| 1 | 1 | 2 | 3 |
| | 8 | 9 | 10 |

| NOTES | SUNDAY | MONDAY | TUESDAY |
|---|---|---|---|
| | 28 | 29 | 30 |
| | 4<br>Easter Sunday<br>Daylight Saving Time ends (AU)<br>Last Quarter ◑ | 5<br>Easter Monday<br>National Library Week begins (U.S.) | 6 |
| | 11 | 12<br>Ramadan (begins at sundown)<br>New Moon ● | 13 |
| | 18 | 19 | 20<br>First Quarter ◐ |
| | 25<br>ANZAC Day (AU, N.Z.) | 26<br>St. George's Day (CA) | 27<br>King's Birthday (NL<br>Full Moon ○ |
| | 2 | 3 | 4 |

MARCH

| S | M | T | W | T | F | S |
|---|---|---|---|---|---|---|
| | 1 | 2 | 3 | 4 | 5 | 6 |
| 7 | 8 | 9 | 10 | 11 | 12 | 13 |
| 14 | 15 | 16 | 17 | 18 | 19 | 20 |
| 21 | 22 | 23 | 24 | 25 | 26 | 27 |
| 28 | 29 | 30 | 31 | | | |

MAY

| S | M | T | W | T | F | S |
|---|---|---|---|---|---|---|
| | | | | | | 1 |
| 2 | 3 | 4 | 5 | 6 | 7 | 8 |
| 9 | 10 | 11 | 12 | 13 | 14 | 15 |
| 16 | 17 | 18 | 19 | 20 | 21 | 22 |
| 23 | 24 | 25 | 26 | 27 | 28 | 29 |
| 30 | 31 | | | | | |

# April 2021

| WEDNESDAY | THURSDAY | FRIDAY | SATURDAY |
|---|---|---|---|
| 1 | 1 April Fools' Day | 2 Good Friday | 3 |
| Holocaust Remembrance Day (begins at sundown) | 8 | 9 | 10 |
| 4 | 15 Income Tax Due (U.S.) | 16 | 17 |
| 1 Administrative ofessionals Day (U.S.) Tiradentes Day (BR) | 22 Earth Day Take Our Daughters and Sons to Work® Day (U.S.) | 23 Shakespeare Day (U.K.) St. George's Day (U.K.) | 24 |
| 8 | 29 | 30 Arbor Day (U.S.) | 1 |
| | 6 | 7 | 8 |

| NOTES | SUNDAY | MONDAY | TUESDAY |
|---|---|---|---|
| | 25 | 26 | 27 |
| | 2<br>Teacher Appreciation Week begins (U.S.) | 3<br>Holiday (U.K., Rep. of Ire.)<br>Labour Day/May Day (AU)<br>Constitution Day (PL)<br>Last Quarter ◑ | 4 |
| | 9<br>Mother's Day (U.S., CA, AU) | 10 | 11<br>New Moon ● |
| | 16<br>Shavuot (begins at sundown) | 17 | 18 |
| | 23<br>Pentecost (Whit Sunday) | 24<br>Whit Monday<br>Victoria Day (CA) | 25 |
| | 30 | 31<br>Memorial Day (U.S.)<br>Holiday (U.K.) | 1 |

APRIL

| S | M | T | W | T | F | S |
|---|---|---|---|---|---|---|
| | | | | 1 | 2 | 3 |
| 4 | 5 | 6 | 7 | 8 | 9 | 10 |
| 11 | 12 | 13 | 14 | 15 | 16 | 17 |
| 18 | 19 | 20 | 21 | 22 | 23 | 24 |
| 25 | 26 | 27 | 28 | 29 | 30 | |

JUNE

| S | M | T | W | T | F | S |
|---|---|---|---|---|---|---|
| | | 1 | 2 | 3 | 4 | 5 |
| 6 | 7 | 8 | 9 | 10 | 11 | 12 |
| 13 | 14 | 15 | 16 | 17 | 18 | 19 |
| 20 | 21 | 22 | 23 | 24 | 25 | 26 |
| 27 | 28 | 29 | 30 | | | |

# May 2021

| VEDNESDAY | THURSDAY | FRIDAY | SATURDAY |
|---|---|---|---|
| 8 | 29 | 30 | 1<br>May Day |
| Cinco de Mayo<br>(U.S., MX)<br>Liberation Day (NL) | 6 | 7 | 8<br>Laylat al-Qadr<br>(begins at sundown) |
| 2<br>Eid al-Fitr<br>begins at sundown)<br>ernational Nurses Day | 13<br>Ascension Day | 14 | 15<br>Armed Forces Day (U.S.) |
| 9<br>First Quarter ◐ | 20 | 21 | 22 |
| 6<br>Full Moon ○ | 27 | 28 | 29 |
| | 3 | 4 | 5 |

| NOTES | SUNDAY | MONDAY | TUESDAY |
|---|---|---|---|
| | 30 | 31 | 1 |
| | 6<br>D-Day | 7<br>Holiday (Rep. of Ire.)<br>Queen's Birthday (N.Z.) | 8 |
| | 13 | 14<br>Flag Day (U.S.)<br>Queen's Birthday (AU) | 15 |
| | 20<br>Father's Day (U.S., CA, U.K.) | 21<br>June Solstice | 22 |
| | 27 | 28 | 29 |
| | 4 | 5 | 6 |

MAY

| S | M | T | W | T | F | S |
|---|---|---|---|---|---|---|
| | | | | | | 1 |
| 2 | 3 | 4 | 5 | 6 | 7 | 8 |
| 9 | 10 | 11 | 12 | 13 | 14 | 15 |
| 16 | 17 | 18 | 19 | 20 | 21 | 22 |
| 23 | 24 | 25 | 26 | 27 | 28 | 29 |
| 30 | 31 | | | | | |

JULY

| S | M | T | W | T | F | S |
|---|---|---|---|---|---|---|
| | | | | 1 | 2 | 3 |
| 4 | 5 | 6 | 7 | 8 | 9 | 10 |
| 11 | 12 | 13 | 14 | 15 | 16 | 17 |
| 18 | 19 | 20 | 21 | 22 | 23 | 24 |
| 25 | 26 | 27 | 28 | 29 | 30 | 31 |

# June 2021

| WEDNESDAY | THURSDAY | FRIDAY | SATURDAY |
|---|---|---|---|
| Last Quarter ◑ | 3 Corpus Christi | 4 | 5 World Environment Day |
| | 10 New Moon ● | 11 | 12 |
| 6 | 17 | 18 First Quarter ◐ | 19 Juneteenth (U.S.) |
| 3 | 24 Full Moon ○ | 25 | 26 |
| o | 1 | 2 | 3 |
| | 8 | 9 | 10 |

| NOTES | SUNDAY | MONDAY | TUESDAY |
|---|---|---|---|
| | 27 | 28 | 29 |
| | 4<br>Independence Day (U.S.)<br>NAIDOC Week begins (AU) | 5<br>Independence Day observed (U.S.) | 6 |
| | 11 | 12<br>Holiday (N. Ire.) | 13 |
| | 18 | 19<br>Eid al-Adha (begins at sundown) | 20 |
| | 25<br>Parents' Day (U.S.) | 26 | 27 |
| | 1 | 2 | 3 |

JUNE

| S | M | T | W | T | F | S |
|---|---|---|---|---|---|---|
| | | 1 | 2 | 3 | 4 | 5 |
| 6 | 7 | 8 | 9 | 10 | 11 | 12 |
| 13 | 14 | 15 | 16 | 17 | 18 | 19 |
| 20 | 21 | 22 | 23 | 24 | 25 | 26 |
| 27 | 28 | 29 | 30 | | | |

AUGUST

| S | M | T | W | T | F | S |
|---|---|---|---|---|---|---|
| 1 | 2 | 3 | 4 | 5 | 6 | 7 |
| 8 | 9 | 10 | 11 | 12 | 13 | 14 |
| 15 | 16 | 17 | 18 | 19 | 20 | 21 |
| 22 | 23 | 24 | 25 | 26 | 27 | 28 |
| 29 | 30 | 31 | | | | |

# July 2021

| WEDNESDAY | THURSDAY | FRIDAY | SATURDAY |
|---|---|---|---|
| 0 | 1<br>Canada Day<br>Last Quarter ◑ | 2 | 3 |
| | 8 | 9 | 10<br>New Moon ● |
| 4<br>Bastille Day (FR) | 15 | 16 | 17<br>First Quarter ◐ |
| 1 | 22 | 23 | 24<br>Full Moon ○ |
| 8 | 29 | 30<br>International Day of Friendship | 31<br>Last Quarter ◑ |
| | 5 | 6 | 7 |

| NOTES | SUNDAY | MONDAY | TUESDAY |
|---|---|---|---|
| | 1<br>Friendship Day (U.S.) | 2<br>Holiday<br>(CA, Scot., Rep. of Ire.) | 3 |
| | 8<br>New Moon ● | 9<br>Al-Hijra<br>(begins at sundown) | 10 |
| | 15<br>Assumption Day<br>First Quarter ◐ | 16 | 17 |
| | 22<br>Full Moon ○ | 23 | 24 |
| | 29 | 30<br>Holiday<br>(Eng., N. Ire., Wales)<br>Last Quarter ◑ | 31 |
| | 5 | 6 | 7 |

JULY

| S | M | T | W | T | F | S |
|---|---|---|---|---|---|---|
| | | | | 1 | 2 | 3 |
| 4 | 5 | 6 | 7 | 8 | 9 | 10 |
| 11 | 12 | 13 | 14 | 15 | 16 | 17 |
| 18 | 19 | 20 | 21 | 22 | 23 | 24 |
| 25 | 26 | 27 | 28 | 29 | 30 | 31 |

SEPTEMBER

| S | M | T | W | T | F | S |
|---|---|---|---|---|---|---|
| | | | 1 | 2 | 3 | 4 |
| 5 | 6 | 7 | 8 | 9 | 10 | 11 |
| 12 | 13 | 14 | 15 | 16 | 17 | 18 |
| 19 | 20 | 21 | 22 | 23 | 24 | 25 |
| 26 | 27 | 28 | 29 | 30 | | |

# August 2021

| WEDNESDAY | THURSDAY | FRIDAY | SATURDAY |
|---|---|---|---|
| 4 | 5 | 6 | 7 |
| 1 | 12<br>International Youth Day | 13 | 14 |
| 8<br>Ashura<br>(begins at sundown) | 19 | 20 | 21<br>Senior Citizens Day<br>(U.S.) |
| 5 | 26<br>Women's Equality Day<br>(U.S.) | 27 | 28 |
| | 2 | 3 | 4 |
| | 9 | 10 | 11 |

| NOTES | SUNDAY | MONDAY | TUESDAY |
|---|---|---|---|
| | 29 | 30 | 31 |
| | 5<br>Father's Day (AU) | 6<br>Rosh Hashanah (begins at sundown)<br>Labor Day (U.S., CA) | 7<br>Independence Day (BR)<br>New Moon ● |
| | 12<br>Grandparents Day (U.S.) | 13<br>First Quarter ◐ | 14 |
| | 19 | 20<br>Sukkot (begins at sundown)<br>Full Moon ○ | 21<br>International Day of Peace |
| | 26 | 27 | 28<br>Simchat Torah (begins at sundown) |
| | 3 | 4 | 5 |

AUGUST

| S | M | T | W | T | F | S |
|---|---|---|---|---|---|---|
| 1 | 2 | 3 | 4 | 5 | 6 | 7 |
| 8 | 9 | 10 | 11 | 12 | 13 | 14 |
| 15 | 16 | 17 | 18 | 19 | 20 | 21 |
| 22 | 23 | 24 | 25 | 26 | 27 | 28 |
| 29 | 30 | 31 | | | | |

OCTOBER

| S | M | T | W | T | F | S |
|---|---|---|---|---|---|---|
| | | | | | 1 | 2 |
| 3 | 4 | 5 | 6 | 7 | 8 | 9 |
| 10 | 11 | 12 | 13 | 14 | 15 | 16 |
| 17 | 18 | 19 | 20 | 21 | 22 | 23 |
| 24 | 25 | 26 | 27 | 28 | 29 | 30 |
| 31 | | | | | | |

# September 2021

| WEDNESDAY | THURSDAY | FRIDAY | SATURDAY |
|---|---|---|---|
| | 2 | 3 | 4 |
| | 9 | 10 | 11<br>Patriot Day (U.S.) |
| 5<br>Yom Kippur (begins at sundown)<br>Start of National Hispanic Heritage Month (U.S.) | 16<br>Independence Day (MX) | 17<br>Constitution Day/ Citizenship Day (U.S.) | 18 |
| 22<br>September Equinox | 23 | 24<br>Native Americans' Day (U.S.) | 25 |
| 29<br>Last Quarter ◑ | 30 | 1 | 2 |
| | 7 | 8 | 9 |

| NOTES | SUNDAY | MONDAY | TUESDAY |
|---|---|---|---|
| | 26 | 27 | 28 |
| | 3<br>Daylight Saving Time begins (AU) | 4<br>Labour Day (AU) | 5 |
| | 10 | 11<br>Columbus Day (U.S.)<br>Thanksgiving Day (CA) | 12<br>Our Lady Aparecida/ Children's Day (BR) |
| | 17 | 18 | 19 |
| | 24<br>United Nations Day | 25<br>Holiday (Rep. of Ire.)<br>Labour Day (N.Z.) | 26 |
| | 31<br>Halloween<br>British/European Summer Time ends | 1 | 2 |

SEPTEMBER

| S | M | T | W | T | F | S |
|---|---|---|---|---|---|---|
| | | | 1 | 2 | 3 | 4 |
| 5 | 6 | 7 | 8 | 9 | 10 | 11 |
| 12 | 13 | 14 | 15 | 16 | 17 | 18 |
| 19 | 20 | 21 | 22 | 23 | 24 | 25 |
| 26 | 27 | 28 | 29 | 30 | | |

NOVEMBER

| S | M | T | W | T | F | S |
|---|---|---|---|---|---|---|
| | 1 | 2 | 3 | 4 | 5 | 6 |
| 7 | 8 | 9 | 10 | 11 | 12 | 13 |
| 14 | 15 | 16 | 17 | 18 | 19 | 20 |
| 21 | 22 | 23 | 24 | 25 | 26 | 27 |
| 28 | 29 | 30 | | | | |

# October 2021

| VEDNESDAY | THURSDAY | FRIDAY | SATURDAY |
| --- | --- | --- | --- |
| 9 | 30 | 1<br>Start of Women's History Month (CA)<br>Start of Black History Month (U.K.) | 2 |
| New Moon ● | 7 | 8 | 9 |
| 3<br>First Quarter ◐ | 14 | 15 | 16 |
| o<br>Full Moon ○ | 21 | 22 | 23 |
| 7 | 28<br>Last Quarter ◑ | 29 | 30 |
| | 4 | 5 | 6 |

| NOTES | SUNDAY | MONDAY | TUESDAY |
|---|---|---|---|
| | 31 | 1<br>All Saints' Day | 2<br>All Souls' Day<br>Election Day (U.S.) |
| | 7<br>Daylight Saving Time ends (U.S., CA) | 8 | 9 |
| | 14<br>Remembrance Sunday (U.K.) | 15<br>Republic Proclamation Day (BR) | 16 |
| | 21 | 22 | 23 |
| | 28<br>Hanukkah (begins at sundown)<br>Advent begins | 29 | 30<br>St. Andrew's Day (Sc |
| | 5 | 6 | 7 |

OCTOBER

| S | M | T | W | T | F | S |
|---|---|---|---|---|---|---|
| | | | | | 1 | 2 |
| 3 | 4 | 5 | 6 | 7 | 8 | 9 |
| 10 | 11 | 12 | 13 | 14 | 15 | 16 |
| 17 | 18 | 19 | 20 | 21 | 22 | 23 |
| 24 | 25 | 26 | 27 | 28 | 29 | 30 |
| 31 | | | | | | |

DECEMBER

| S | M | T | W | T | F | S |
|---|---|---|---|---|---|---|
| | | | 1 | 2 | 3 | 4 |
| 5 | 6 | 7 | 8 | 9 | 10 | 11 |
| 12 | 13 | 14 | 15 | 16 | 17 | 18 |
| 19 | 20 | 21 | 22 | 23 | 24 | 25 |
| 26 | 27 | 28 | 29 | 30 | 31 | |

# November 2021

| WEDNESDAY | THURSDAY | FRIDAY | SATURDAY |
|---|---|---|---|
| ake Our Kids to Work™ Day (CA) | 4<br>New Moon ● | 5<br>Guy Fawkes Night (U.K.) | 6 |
| 0 | 11<br>Veterans Day (U.S.)<br>Remembrance Day (CA, U.K., AU)<br>Armistice Day (FR, N.Z.)<br>Independence Day (PL)<br>First Quarter ◐ | 12 | 13 |
| 7 | 18 | 19<br>Full Moon ○ | 20<br>Universal Children's Day<br>Revolution Day (MX) |
| 4 | 25<br>Thanksgiving Day (U.S.) | 26 | 27<br>Last Quarter ◑ |
| | 2 | 3 | 4 |
| | 9 | 10 | 11 |

| NOTES | SUNDAY | MONDAY | TUESDAY |
| --- | --- | --- | --- |
| | 28 | 29 | 30 |
| | 5 | 6 | 7<br>Pearl Harbor Remembrance Day (U.S.) |
| | 12 | 13 | 14 |
| | 19<br>Full Moon ○ | 20 | 21<br>December Solstice |
| | 26<br>First Day of Kwanzaa<br>Boxing Day<br>Second Day of Christmas (NL, PL)<br>St. Stephen's Day | 27<br>Last Quarter ◑ | 28 |
| | 2 | 3 | 4 |

NOVEMBER

| S | M | T | W | T | F | S |
| --- | --- | --- | --- | --- | --- | --- |
| | 1 | 2 | 3 | 4 | 5 | 6 |
| 7 | 8 | 9 | 10 | 11 | 12 | 13 |
| 14 | 15 | 16 | 17 | 18 | 19 | 20 |
| 21 | 22 | 23 | 24 | 25 | 26 | 27 |
| 28 | 29 | 30 | | | | |

JANUARY 2022

| S | M | T | W | T | F | S |
| --- | --- | --- | --- | --- | --- | --- |
| | | | | | | 1 |
| 2 | 3 | 4 | 5 | 6 | 7 | 8 |
| 9 | 10 | 11 | 12 | 13 | 14 | 15 |
| 16 | 17 | 18 | 19 | 20 | 21 | 22 |
| 23 | 24 | 25 | 26 | 27 | 28 | 29 |
| 30 | 31 | | | | | |

# December 2021

| WEDNESDAY | THURSDAY | FRIDAY | SATURDAY |
|---|---|---|---|
| World AIDS Day | 2 | 3 | 4 New Moon |
| mmaculate Conception | 9 | 10 Human Rights Day | 11 First Quarter |
| 5 | 16 | 17 | 18 |
| 2 | 23 | 24 Christmas Eve | 25 Christmas Day |
| 9 | 30 | 31 New Year's Eve | 1 |
| | 6 | 7 | 8 |

| NOTES | SUNDAY | MONDAY | TUESDAY |
|---|---|---|---|
| | 26 | 27 | 28 |
| | 2<br>New Moon ● | 3<br>New Year's Day observed (CA, U.K., AU, N.Z.) | 4<br>Holiday (Scot., N.Z.) |
| | 9<br>First Quarter ◐ | 10 | 11 |
| | 16 | 17<br>Martin Luther King, Jr. Day (U.S.)<br>Full Moon ○ | 18 |
| | 23 | 24 | 25<br>Burns' Night (Scot.)<br>Last Quarter ◑ |
| | 30 | 31 | 1 |

DECEMBER 2021

| S | M | T | W | T | F | S |
|---|---|---|---|---|---|---|
| | | | 1 | 2 | 3 | 4 |
| 5 | 6 | 7 | 8 | 9 | 10 | 11 |
| 12 | 13 | 14 | 15 | 16 | 17 | 18 |
| 19 | 20 | 21 | 22 | 23 | 24 | 25 |
| 26 | 27 | 28 | 29 | 30 | 31 | |

FEBRUARY

| S | M | T | W | T | F | S |
|---|---|---|---|---|---|---|
| | | 1 | 2 | 3 | 4 | 5 |
| 6 | 7 | 8 | 9 | 10 | 11 | 12 |
| 13 | 14 | 15 | 16 | 17 | 18 | 19 |
| 20 | 21 | 22 | 23 | 24 | 25 | 26 |
| 27 | 28 | | | | | |

# January 2022

| WEDNESDAY | THURSDAY | FRIDAY | SATURDAY |
|---|---|---|---|
| 29 | 30 | 31 | 1<br>New Year's Day |
| 5 | 6<br>Epiphany | 7<br>Orthodox Christmas Day | 8 |
| 12 | 13 | 14<br>Orthodox New Year | 15 |
| 19 | 20 | 21 | 22 |
| 26<br>Australia Day | 27 | 28 | 29 |
| 2 | 3 | 4 | 5 |

| NOTES | SUNDAY | MONDAY | TUESDAY |
|---|---|---|---|
| | 30 | 31 | 1 Chinese New Year begins (Year of the Tiger) Start of Black History Month (U.S., CA) National Freedom Day (U.S.) New Moon ● |
| | 6 Super Bowl Sunday (U.S.) Waitangi Day (N.Z.) | 7 Waitangi Day observed (N.Z.) Constitution Day observed (MX) | 8 First Quarter ◐ |
| | 13 | 14 Valentine's Day | 15 |
| | 20 | 21 Presidents' Day/ Washington's Birthday (U.S.) | 22 |
| | 27 | 28 | 1 |
| | 6 | 7 | 8 |

JANUARY

| S | M | T | W | T | F | S |
|---|---|---|---|---|---|---|
| | | | | | | 1 |
| 2 | 3 | 4 | 5 | 6 | 7 | 8 |
| 9 | 10 | 11 | 12 | 13 | 14 | 15 |
| 16 | 17 | 18 | 19 | 20 | 21 | 22 |
| 23 | 24 | 25 | 26 | 27 | 28 | 29 |
| 30 | 31 | | | | | |

MARCH

| S | M | T | W | T | F | S |
|---|---|---|---|---|---|---|
| | | 1 | 2 | 3 | 4 | 5 |
| 6 | 7 | 8 | 9 | 10 | 11 | 12 |
| 13 | 14 | 15 | 16 | 17 | 18 | 19 |
| 20 | 21 | 22 | 23 | 24 | 25 | 26 |
| 27 | 28 | 29 | 30 | 31 | | |

# February 2022

| VEDNESDAY | THURSDAY | FRIDAY | SATURDAY |
| --- | --- | --- | --- |
| Groundhog Day (U.S., CA) | 3 | 4 | 5<br>Constitution Day (MX) |
| | 10 | 11<br>Lincoln's Birthday observed (U.S.) | 12<br>Lincoln's Birthday (U.S.) |
| 6<br>Full Moon ○ | 17 | 18 | 19 |
| 3<br>Last Quarter ◑ | 24 | 25 | 26 |
| | 3 | 4 | 5 |
| | 10 | 11 | 12 |

| NOTES | SUNDAY | MONDAY | TUESDAY |
|---|---|---|---|
| | 27 | 28 | 1<br>Start of Women's Hist<br>Month (U.S., U.K., A<br>Shrove Tuesday/ Mardi Gras<br>St. David's Day |
| | 6 | 7 | 8<br>International Women's Day |
| | 13<br>Daylight Saving Time begins (U.S., CA) | 14<br>Commonwealth Day (CA, U.K., AU) | 15 |
| | 20<br>March Equinox | 21 | 22 |
| | 27<br>British/European Summer Time begins<br>Mother's Day (U.K., Rep. of Ire.) | 28 | 29 |
| | 3 | 4 | 5 |

FEBRUARY

| S | M | T | W | T | F | S |
|---|---|---|---|---|---|---|
| | | 1 | 2 | 3 | 4 | 5 |
| 6 | 7 | 8 | 9 | 10 | 11 | 12 |
| 13 | 14 | 15 | 16 | 17 | 18 | 19 |
| 20 | 21 | 22 | 23 | 24 | 25 | 26 |
| 27 | 28 | | | | | |

APRIL

| S | M | T | W | T | F | S |
|---|---|---|---|---|---|---|
| | | | | | 1 | 2 |
| 3 | 4 | 5 | 6 | 7 | 8 | 9 |
| 10 | 11 | 12 | 13 | 14 | 15 | 16 |
| 17 | 18 | 19 | 20 | 21 | 22 | 23 |
| 24 | 25 | 26 | 27 | 28 | 29 | 30 |

# March 2022

| WEDNESDAY | THURSDAY | FRIDAY | SATURDAY |
|---|---|---|---|
| Ash Wednesday<br>New Moon ● | 3 | 4 | 5 |
|  | 10<br>First Quarter ◐ | 11 | 12 |
| 6 | 17<br>Purim (begins at sundown)<br>St. Patrick's Day | 18<br>Full Moon ○ | 19 |
| 3 | 24 | 25<br>Last Quarter ◑ | 26 |
| 0 | 31 | 1 | 2 |
|  | 7 | 8 | 9 |

| NOTES | SUNDAY | MONDAY | TUESDAY |
|---|---|---|---|
| | 27 | 28 | 29 |
| | 3<br>Daylight Saving Time ends (AU) | 4 | 5 |
| | 10<br>Palm Sunday<br>National Library Week begins (U.S.) | 11 | 12 |
| | 17<br>Easter Sunday | 18<br>Easter Monday<br>Income Tax Due (U.S.) | 19 |
| | 24 | 25<br>St. George's Day (CA)<br>ANZAC Day (AU, N.Z.) | 26 |
| | 1 | 2 | 3 |

MARCH

| S | M | T | W | T | F | S |
|---|---|---|---|---|---|---|
| | | 1 | 2 | 3 | 4 | 5 |
| 6 | 7 | 8 | 9 | 10 | 11 | 12 |
| 13 | 14 | 15 | 16 | 17 | 18 | 19 |
| 20 | 21 | 22 | 23 | 24 | 25 | 26 |
| 27 | 28 | 29 | 30 | 31 | | |

MAY

| S | M | T | W | T | F | S |
|---|---|---|---|---|---|---|
| 1 | 2 | 3 | 4 | 5 | 6 | 7 |
| 8 | 9 | 10 | 11 | 12 | 13 | 14 |
| 15 | 16 | 17 | 18 | 19 | 20 | 21 |
| 22 | 23 | 24 | 25 | 26 | 27 | 28 |
| 29 | 30 | 31 | | | | |

# April 2022

| WEDNESDAY | THURSDAY | FRIDAY | SATURDAY |
|---|---|---|---|
| 30 | 31 | 1<br>April Fools' Day<br>New Moon ● | 2<br>Ramadan<br>(begins at sundown) |
| 6 | 7 | 8 | 9<br>First Quarter ◐ |
| 13 | 14 | 15<br>Good Friday<br>Passover<br>(begins at sundown) | 16<br>Full Moon ○ |
| 20 | 21<br>Tiradentes Day (BR) | 22<br>Earth Day | 23<br>Shakespeare Day (U.K.)<br>St. George's Day (U.K.)<br>Last Quarter ◑ |
| 27 Holocaust Remembrance Day<br>(begins at sundown)<br>Laylat al-Qadr<br>(begins at sundown)<br>Administrative Professionals Day (U.S.)<br>King's Birthday (NL) | 28<br>Take Our Daughters and Sons to Work® Day<br>(U.S.) | 29<br>Arbor Day (U.S.) | 30<br>New Moon ● |
| 4 | 5 | 6 | 7 |

| SUNDAY | MONDAY | TUESDAY |
|---|---|---|
| 1<br>May Day | 2<br>Eid al-Fitr (begins at sundown)<br>Teacher Appreciation Week begins (U.S.)<br>Holiday (U.K., Rep. of Ire.)<br>Labour Day/May Day (AU) | 3<br>Constitution Day (PL) |
| 8<br>Mother's Day (U.S., CA, AU) | 9<br>First Quarter ◐ | 10 |
| 15 | 16<br>Full Moon ○ | 17 |
| 22<br>Last Quarter ◑ | 23<br>Victoria Day (CA) | 24 |
| 29 | 30<br>Memorial Day (U.S.)<br>Holiday (U.K.)<br>New Moon ● | 31 |
| 5 | 6 | 7 |

NOTES

APRIL

| S | M | T | W | T | F | S |
|---|---|---|---|---|---|---|
| | | | | | 1 | 2 |
| 3 | 4 | 5 | 6 | 7 | 8 | 9 |
| 10 | 11 | 12 | 13 | 14 | 15 | 16 |
| 17 | 18 | 19 | 20 | 21 | 22 | 23 |
| 24 | 25 | 26 | 27 | 28 | 29 | 30 |

JUNE

| S | M | T | W | T | F | S |
|---|---|---|---|---|---|---|
| | | | 1 | 2 | 3 | 4 |
| 5 | 6 | 7 | 8 | 9 | 10 | 11 |
| 12 | 13 | 14 | 15 | 16 | 17 | 18 |
| 19 | 20 | 21 | 22 | 23 | 24 | 25 |
| 26 | 27 | 28 | 29 | 30 | | |

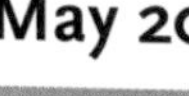

# May 2022

| WEDNESDAY | THURSDAY | FRIDAY | SATURDAY |
|---|---|---|---|
| 4 | 5<br>Cinco de Mayo (U.S., MX)<br>Liberation Day (NL) | 6 | 7 |
| 1 | 12<br>International Nurses Day | 13 | 14 |
| 8 | 19 | 20 | 21<br>Armed Forces Day (U.S.) |
| 5 | 26<br>Ascension Day | 27 | 28 |
|  | 2 | 3 | 4 |
| 3 | 9 | 10 | 11 |

| NOTES | SUNDAY | MONDAY | TUESDAY |
|---|---|---|---|
| | 29 | 30 | 31 |
| | 5<br>World Environment Day<br>Pentecost (Whit Sunday) | 6<br>Whit Monday<br>D-Day<br>Holiday (Rep. of Ire.)<br>Queen's Birthday (N.Z.) | 7<br>First Quarter ◐ |
| | 12 | 13<br>Queen's Birthday (AU) | 14<br>Flag Day (U.S.)<br>Full Moon ○ |
| | 19<br>Father's Day (U.S., CA, U.K.)<br>Juneteenth (U.S.) | 20 | 21<br>June Solstice<br>Last Quarter ◑ |
| | 26 | 27 | 28 |
| | 3 | 4 | 5 |

MAY

| S | M | T | W | T | F | S |
|---|---|---|---|---|---|---|
| 1 | 2 | 3 | 4 | 5 | 6 | 7 |
| 8 | 9 | 10 | 11 | 12 | 13 | 14 |
| 15 | 16 | 17 | 18 | 19 | 20 | 21 |
| 22 | 23 | 24 | 25 | 26 | 27 | 28 |
| 29 | 30 | 31 | | | | |

JULY

| S | M | T | W | T | F | S |
|---|---|---|---|---|---|---|
| | | | | | 1 | 2 |
| 3 | 4 | 5 | 6 | 7 | 8 | 9 |
| 10 | 11 | 12 | 13 | 14 | 15 | 16 |
| 17 | 18 | 19 | 20 | 21 | 22 | 23 |
| 24 | 25 | 26 | 27 | 28 | 29 | 30 |
| 31 | | | | | | |

# June 2022

| WEDNESDAY | THURSDAY | FRIDAY | SATURDAY |
|---|---|---|---|
| | 2 | 3 | 4<br>Shavuot<br>(begins at sundown) |
| | 9 | 10 | 11 |
| 5 | 16<br>Corpus Christi | 17 | 18 |
| 2 | 23 | 24 | 25 |
| 9<br>New Moon ● | 30 | 1 | 2 |
| | 7 | 8 | 9 |

| NOTES | SUNDAY | MONDAY | TUESDAY |
|---|---|---|---|
| | 26 | 27 | 28 |
| | 3<br>NAIDOC Week begins (AU) | 4<br>Independence Day (U.S.) | 5 |
| | 10 | 11 | 12<br>Holiday (N. Ire.) |
| | 17 | 18 | 19 |
| | 24<br>Parents' Day (U.S.) | 25 | 26 |
| | 31 | 1 | 2 |

JUNE

| S | M | T | W | T | F | S |
|---|---|---|---|---|---|---|
| | | | 1 | 2 | 3 | 4 |
| 5 | 6 | 7 | 8 | 9 | 10 | 11 |
| 12 | 13 | 14 | 15 | 16 | 17 | 18 |
| 19 | 20 | 21 | 22 | 23 | 24 | 25 |
| 26 | 27 | 28 | 29 | 30 | | |

AUGUST

| S | M | T | W | T | F | S |
|---|---|---|---|---|---|---|
| | 1 | 2 | 3 | 4 | 5 | 6 |
| 7 | 8 | 9 | 10 | 11 | 12 | 13 |
| 14 | 15 | 16 | 17 | 18 | 19 | 20 |
| 21 | 22 | 23 | 24 | 25 | 26 | 27 |
| 28 | 29 | 30 | 31 | | | |

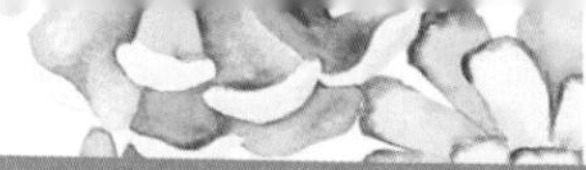

# July 2022

| /EDNESDAY | THURSDAY | FRIDAY | SATURDAY |
|---|---|---|---|
| 9 | 30 | 1<br>Canada Day | 2 |
| | 7<br>First Quarter ◐ | 8 | 9<br>Eid al-Adha (begins at sundown) |
| 3<br>Full Moon ○ | 14<br>Bastille Day (FR) | 15 | 16 |
| O<br>Last Quarter ◑ | 21 | 22 | 23 |
| 7 | 28<br>New Moon ● | 29<br>Al-Hijra (begins at sundown) | 30<br>International Day of Friendship |
| | 4 | 5 | 6 |

| NOTES | SUNDAY | MONDAY | TUESDAY |
|---|---|---|---|
| | 31 | 1<br>Holiday<br>(CA, Scot., Rep. of Ire.) | 2 |
| | 7<br>Ashura<br>(begins at sundown)<br>Friendship Day (U.S.) | 8 | 9 |
| | 14 | 15<br>Assumption Day | 16 |
| | 21<br>Senior Citizens Day<br>(U.S.) | 22 | 23 |
| | 28 | 29<br>Holiday<br>(Eng., N. Ire., Wales) | 30 |
| | 4 | 5 | 6 |

JULY

| S | M | T | W | T | F | S |
|---|---|---|---|---|---|---|
| | | | | | 1 | 2 |
| 3 | 4 | 5 | 6 | 7 | 8 | 9 |
| 10 | 11 | 12 | 13 | 14 | 15 | 16 |
| 17 | 18 | 19 | 20 | 21 | 22 | 23 |
| 24 | 25 | 26 | 27 | 28 | 29 | 30 |
| 31 | | | | | | |

SEPTEMBER

| S | M | T | W | T | F | S |
|---|---|---|---|---|---|---|
| | | | | 1 | 2 | 3 |
| 4 | 5 | 6 | 7 | 8 | 9 | 10 |
| 11 | 12 | 13 | 14 | 15 | 16 | 17 |
| 18 | 19 | 20 | 21 | 22 | 23 | 24 |
| 25 | 26 | 27 | 28 | 29 | 30 | |

# August 2022

| VEDNESDAY | THURSDAY | FRIDAY | SATURDAY |
|---|---|---|---|
| | 4 | 5<br>First Quarter ◐ | 6 |
| 0 | 11 | 12<br>International Youth Day<br>Full Moon ○ | 13 |
| 7 | 18 | 19<br>Last Quarter ◑ | 20 |
| 4 | 25 | 26<br>Women's Equality Day (U.S.) | 27<br>New Moon ● |
| 1 | 1 | 2 | 3 |
| | 8 | 9 | 10 |

| NOTES | SUNDAY | MONDAY | TUESDAY |
|---|---|---|---|
| | 28 | 29 | 30 |
| | 4<br>Father's Day (AU) | 5<br>Labor Day (U.S., CA) | 6 |
| | 11<br>Grandparents Day (U.S.)<br>Patriot Day (U.S.) | 12 | 13 |
| | 18 | 19 | 20 |
| | 25<br>Rosh Hashanah (begins at sundown)<br>New Moon ● | 26 | 27 |
| | 2 | 3 | 4 |

AUGUST

| S | M | T | W | T | F | S |
|---|---|---|---|---|---|---|
| | 1 | 2 | 3 | 4 | 5 | 6 |
| 7 | 8 | 9 | 10 | 11 | 12 | 13 |
| 14 | 15 | 16 | 17 | 18 | 19 | 20 |
| 21 | 22 | 23 | 24 | 25 | 26 | 27 |
| 28 | 29 | 30 | 31 | | | |

OCTOBER

| S | M | T | W | T | F | S |
|---|---|---|---|---|---|---|
| | | | | | | 1 |
| 2 | 3 | 4 | 5 | 6 | 7 | 8 |
| 9 | 10 | 11 | 12 | 13 | 14 | 15 |
| 16 | 17 | 18 | 19 | 20 | 21 | 22 |
| 23 | 24 | 25 | 26 | 27 | 28 | 29 |
| 30 | 31 | | | | | |

# September 2022

| WEDNESDAY | THURSDAY | FRIDAY | SATURDAY |
|---|---|---|---|
| 1 | 1 | 2 | 3<br>First Quarter ◐ |
| ndependence Day (BR) | 8 | 9 | 10<br>Full Moon ○ |
| 4 | 15<br>Start of National Hispanic Heritage Month (U.S.) | 16<br>Constitution Day/ Citizenship Day observed (U.S.)<br>Independence Day (MX) | 17<br>Constitution Day/ Citizenship Day (U.S.)<br>Last Quarter ◑ |
| 1<br>International Day of Peace | 22<br>September Equinox | 23<br>Native Americans' Day (U.S.) | 24 |
| 8 | 29 | 30 | 1 |
|  | 6 | 7 | 8 |

| NOTES | SUNDAY | MONDAY | TUESDAY |
|---|---|---|---|
| | 25 | 26 | 27 |
| | 2<br>Daylight Saving Time begins (AU) | 3<br>Labour Day (AU)<br>First Quarter ◐ | 4<br>Yom Kippur (begins at sundown) |
| | 9<br>Sukkot (begins at sundown)<br>Full Moon ○ | 10<br>Columbus Day (U.S.)<br>Thanksgiving Day (CA) | 11 |
| | 16 | 17<br>Simchat Torah (begins at sundown)<br>Last Quarter ◑ | 18 |
| | 23 | 24<br>United Nations Day<br>Labour Day (N.Z.) | 25<br>New Moon ● |
| | 30<br>British/European Summer Time ends | 31<br>Halloween<br>Holiday (Rep. of Ire.) | 1 |

SEPTEMBER

| S | M | T | W | T | F | S |
|---|---|---|---|---|---|---|
| | | | | 1 | 2 | 3 |
| 4 | 5 | 6 | 7 | 8 | 9 | 10 |
| 11 | 12 | 13 | 14 | 15 | 16 | 17 |
| 18 | 19 | 20 | 21 | 22 | 23 | 24 |
| 25 | 26 | 27 | 28 | 29 | 30 | |

NOVEMBER

| S | M | T | W | T | F | S |
|---|---|---|---|---|---|---|
| | | 1 | 2 | 3 | 4 | 5 |
| 6 | 7 | 8 | 9 | 10 | 11 | 12 |
| 13 | 14 | 15 | 16 | 17 | 18 | 19 |
| 20 | 21 | 22 | 23 | 24 | 25 | 26 |
| 27 | 28 | 29 | 30 | | | |

# October 2022

| EDNESDAY | THURSDAY | FRIDAY | SATURDAY |
|---|---|---|---|
| 8 | 29 | 30 | 1<br>Start of Women's History Month (CA)<br>Start of Black History Month (U.K.) |
| | 6 | 7 | 8 |
| 2<br>ur Lady Aparecida/<br>hildren's Day (BR) | 13 | 14 | 15 |
| 9 | 20 | 21 | 22 |
| 6 | 27 | 28 | 29 |
| | 3 | 4 | 5 |

| NOTES | SUNDAY | MONDAY | TUESDAY |
|---|---|---|---|
| | 30 | 31 | 1<br>All Saints' Day<br>First Quarter ◐ |
| | 6<br>Daylight Saving Time ends (U.S., CA) | 7 | 8<br>Election Day (U.S.<br>Full Moon ○ |
| | 13<br>Remembrance Sunday (U.K.) | 14 | 15<br>Republic Proclamat Day (BR) |
| | 20<br>Universal Children's Day<br>Revolution Day (MX) | 21 | 22 |
| | 27<br>Advent begins | 28 | 29 |
| | 4 | 5 | 6 |

OCTOBER

| S | M | T | W | T | F | S |
|---|---|---|---|---|---|---|
| | | | | | | 1 |
| 2 | 3 | 4 | 5 | 6 | 7 | 8 |
| 9 | 10 | 11 | 12 | 13 | 14 | 15 |
| 16 | 17 | 18 | 19 | 20 | 21 | 22 |
| 23 | 24 | 25 | 26 | 27 | 28 | 29 |
| 30 | 31 | | | | | |

DECEMBER

| S | M | T | W | T | F | S |
|---|---|---|---|---|---|---|
| | | | | 1 | 2 | 3 |
| 4 | 5 | 6 | 7 | 8 | 9 | 10 |
| 11 | 12 | 13 | 14 | 15 | 16 | 17 |
| 18 | 19 | 20 | 21 | 22 | 23 | 24 |
| 25 | 26 | 27 | 28 | 29 | 30 | 31 |

# November 2022

| EDNESDAY | THURSDAY | FRIDAY | SATURDAY |
|---|---|---|---|
| All Souls' Day<br>e Our Kids to Work™ Day (CA) | 3 | 4 | 5<br>Guy Fawkes Night (U.K.) |
| | 10 | 11<br>Veterans Day (U.S.)<br>Remembrance Day (CA, U.K., AU)<br>Armistice Day (FR, N.Z.)<br>Independence Day (PL) | 12 |
| 6<br>Last Quarter ◑ | 17 | 18 | 19 |
| 3<br>New Moon ● | 24<br>Thanksgiving Day (U.S.) | 25 | 26 |
| 0<br>Andrew's Day (Scot.)<br>First Quarter ◐ | 1 | 2 | 3 |
| | 8 | 9 | 10 |

| NOTES | SUNDAY | MONDAY | TUESDAY |
|---|---|---|---|
| | 27 | 28 | 29 |
| | 4 | 5 | 6 |
| | 11 | 12 | 13 |
| | 18<br>Hanukkah (begins at sundown) | 19 | 20 |
| | 25<br>Christmas Day | 26<br>Christmas Day observed<br>First Day of Kwanzaa<br>Boxing Day<br>Second Day of Christmas (NL, PL)<br>St. Stephen's Day | 27 |
| | 1 | 2 | 3 |

NOVEMBER

| S | M | T | W | T | F | S |
|---|---|---|---|---|---|---|
| | | 1 | 2 | 3 | 4 | 5 |
| 6 | 7 | 8 | 9 | 10 | 11 | 12 |
| 13 | 14 | 15 | 16 | 17 | 18 | 19 |
| 20 | 21 | 22 | 23 | 24 | 25 | 26 |
| 27 | 28 | 29 | 30 | | | |

JANUARY 2023

| S | M | T | W | T | F | S |
|---|---|---|---|---|---|---|
| 1 | 2 | 3 | 4 | 5 | 6 | 7 |
| 8 | 9 | 10 | 11 | 12 | 13 | 14 |
| 15 | 16 | 17 | 18 | 19 | 20 | 21 |
| 22 | 23 | 24 | 25 | 26 | 27 | 28 |
| 29 | 30 | 31 | | | | |

# December 2022

| EDNESDAY | THURSDAY | FRIDAY | SATURDAY |
|---|---|---|---|
| | 1<br>World AIDS Day | 2 | 3 |
| Pearl Harbor<br>Remembrance Day<br>(U.S.) | 8<br>Immaculate Conception<br>Full Moon ○ | 9 | 10<br>Human Rights Day |
| 4 | 15 | 16<br>Last Quarter ◑ | 17 |
| December Solstice | 22 | 23<br>New Moon ● | 24<br>Christmas Eve |
| 8 | 29 | 30<br>First Quarter ◐ | 31<br>New Year's Eve |
| | 5 | 6 | 7 |

# • 2023 •

## January 2023

| S | M | T | W | T | F | S |
|---|---|---|---|---|---|---|
| 1 | 2 | 3 | 4 | 5 | 6 | 7 |
| 8 | 9 | 10 | 11 | 12 | 13 | 14 |
| 15 | 16 | 17 | 18 | 19 | 20 | 21 |
| 22 | 23 | 24 | 25 | 26 | 27 | 28 |
| 29 | 30 | 31 | | | | |

## February 2023

| S | M | T | W | T | F | S |
|---|---|---|---|---|---|---|
| | | | 1 | 2 | 3 | 4 |
| 5 | 6 | 7 | 8 | 9 | 10 | 11 |
| 12 | 13 | 14 | 15 | 16 | 17 | 18 |
| 19 | 20 | 21 | 22 | 23 | 24 | 25 |
| 26 | 27 | 28 | | | | |

## March 2023

| S | M | T | W | T | F | S |
|---|---|---|---|---|---|---|
| | | | 1 | 2 | 3 | 4 |
| 5 | 6 | 7 | 8 | 9 | 10 | 11 |
| 12 | 13 | 14 | 15 | 16 | 17 | 18 |
| 19 | 20 | 21 | 22 | 23 | 24 | 25 |
| 26 | 27 | 28 | 29 | 30 | 31 | |

## April 2023

| S | M | T | W | T | F | S |
|---|---|---|---|---|---|---|
| | | | | | | 1 |
| 2 | 3 | 4 | 5 | 6 | 7 | 8 |
| 9 | 10 | 11 | 12 | 13 | 14 | 15 |
| 16 | 17 | 18 | 19 | 20 | 21 | 22 |
| 23/30 | 24 | 25 | 26 | 27 | 28 | 29 |

## May 2023

| S | M | T | W | T | F | S |
|---|---|---|---|---|---|---|
| | 1 | 2 | 3 | 4 | 5 | 6 |
| 7 | 8 | 9 | 10 | 11 | 12 | 13 |
| 14 | 15 | 16 | 17 | 18 | 19 | 20 |
| 21 | 22 | 23 | 24 | 25 | 26 | 27 |
| 28 | 29 | 30 | 31 | | | |

## June 2023

| S | M | T | W | T | F | S |
|---|---|---|---|---|---|---|
| | | | | 1 | 2 | 3 |
| 4 | 5 | 6 | 7 | 8 | 9 | 10 |
| 11 | 12 | 13 | 14 | 15 | 16 | 17 |
| 18 | 19 | 20 | 21 | 22 | 23 | 24 |
| 25 | 26 | 27 | 28 | 29 | 30 | |

## July 2023

| S | M | T | W | T | F | S |
|---|---|---|---|---|---|---|
| | | | | | | 1 |
| 2 | 3 | 4 | 5 | 6 | 7 | 8 |
| 9 | 10 | 11 | 12 | 13 | 14 | 15 |
| 16 | 17 | 18 | 19 | 20 | 21 | 22 |
| 23/30 | 24/31 | 25 | 26 | 27 | 28 | 29 |

## August 2023

| S | M | T | W | T | F | S |
|---|---|---|---|---|---|---|
| | | 1 | 2 | 3 | 4 | 5 |
| 6 | 7 | 8 | 9 | 10 | 11 | 12 |
| 13 | 14 | 15 | 16 | 17 | 18 | 19 |
| 20 | 21 | 22 | 23 | 24 | 25 | 26 |
| 27 | 28 | 29 | 30 | 31 | | |

## September 2023

| S | M | T | W | T | F | S |
|---|---|---|---|---|---|---|
| | | | | | 1 | 2 |
| 3 | 4 | 5 | 6 | 7 | 8 | 9 |
| 10 | 11 | 12 | 13 | 14 | 15 | 16 |
| 17 | 18 | 19 | 20 | 21 | 22 | 23 |
| 24 | 25 | 26 | 27 | 28 | 29 | 30 |

## October 2023

| S | M | T | W | T | F | S |
|---|---|---|---|---|---|---|
| 1 | 2 | 3 | 4 | 5 | 6 | 7 |
| 8 | 9 | 10 | 11 | 12 | 13 | 14 |
| 15 | 16 | 17 | 18 | 19 | 20 | 21 |
| 22 | 23 | 24 | 25 | 26 | 27 | 28 |
| 29 | 30 | 31 | | | | |

## November 2023

| S | M | T | W | T | F | S |
|---|---|---|---|---|---|---|
| | | | 1 | 2 | 3 | 4 |
| 5 | 6 | 7 | 8 | 9 | 10 | 11 |
| 12 | 13 | 14 | 15 | 16 | 17 | 18 |
| 19 | 20 | 21 | 22 | 23 | 24 | 25 |
| 26 | 27 | 28 | 29 | 30 | | |

## December 2023

| S | M | T | W | T | F | S |
|---|---|---|---|---|---|---|
| | | | | | 1 | 2 |
| 3 | 4 | 5 | 6 | 7 | 8 | 9 |
| 10 | 11 | 12 | 13 | 14 | 15 | 16 |
| 17 | 18 | 19 | 20 | 21 | 22 | 23 |
| 24/31 | 25 | 26 | 27 | 28 | 29 | 30 |

# BIRTHDAYS, ANNIVERSARIES, AND DATES TO REMEMBER

**PETER PAUPER PRESS**
*Fine Books and Gifts Since 1928*

## *Our Company*

In 1928, at the age of twenty-two, Peter Beilenson began printing books on a small press in the basement of his parents' home in Larchmont, New York. Peter—and later, his wife, Edna—sought to create fine books that sold at "prices even a pauper could afford."

Today, still family owned and operated, Peter Pauper Press continues to honor our founders' legacy—and our customers' expectations—of beauty, quality, and value.

Illustration by Clare Lake for Jane Mosse Designs

Design by Margaret Rubiano

202 Mamaroneck Avenue
White Plains, NY 10601 USA

ISBN 978-1-4413-3354-4
Printed in China
7 6 5 4 3 2 1
Visit us at www.peterpauper.com

All moon phases, solstices, and equinoxes are based on Coordinated Universal Time (UTC). All religious holidays have been verified to the best of our ability; please be aware that certain holidays may be observed at different times in different regions. While we have made every effort to ensure the accuracy of the information presented in this calendar, we cannot be held liable for any errors, omissions, or inconsistencies.